AYRTON
SENNA

A PERSONAL TRIBUTE

AYRTON SENNA

A PERSONAL TRIBUTE

KEITH SUTTON

Foreword by
Martin Brundle

OSPREY
AUTOMOTIVE

DEDICATION

To my parents, Maurice and Dawn Sutton for their support and encouragement always.

In Memory of Ayrton Senna da Silva, 21 March 1960-1 May 1994; Roland Ratzenberger, 4 July 1962-30 April 1994 and Masako Tsuji, 11 November 1957-23 June 1994

Three friends, departed in 1994, who inspired and touched my life and career.

ACKNOWLEDGMENTS

This book is offered in gratitude to the memory of a man whose talent and personality touched millions of people throughout the world. Privileged as I was to play a small part in that life, I wanted to share some of the joyful moments with as many of Ayrton's fans as possible. Although I did not know it at the time the preparations for this book started in March 1981, when I met the man who would influence all my years as a motorsport photographer.

None of this would have been possible without the unselfish support of the people who encouraged the obsession for motor racing which has been with me since I was a child. Although I cannot mention all their names, they know who they are; I embrace them and thank them all from the bottom of my heart. Thanks go to all my family, to my parents Maurice and Dawn Sutton who encouraged me and supported me through the good and the bad times. To my fiancee Tracey Bradbury whose love, patience and understanding have been a tower of strength.

To my brothers, Mark and Paul, both photographers who are an essential part of Sutton Photographic along with Kate, Tootall, Gavin and Tim. Their hard work has made Sutton Photographic the success which it is today.

Particular thanks go to the people whose friendship and professionalism I have relied on so many times. Steven Tee, Martyn Elford for the shared hire cars. John Townsend for making the early years so much fun. Lynden Swainston and Colin Burr for making travelling around the world less stressful and sometimes comfortable.

Mike Doodson for his literary assistance; and to my bank manager at Lloyds. Howard Ames for his faith and belief in me and my plans.

There are others upon whose friendship I have been able to rely with confidence over many years. My business advisers and friends, Simon Woodhams and John Brooks, who have advised in business matters from experience in their own careers.

To all my friends from Manchester, my home town, who have enabled me to forget motorsport occasionally.

To my Japanese associates, Massa Okikura, Yoshiro Asama and all my Sony family, 'domo arigato'.

To all the motorsport photographers around the world who supply such excellent photographic material to Sutton Photographic. To all of the drivers, team managers, mechanics and journalists who have contributed to this book, no matter how, I offer my thanks. I value their friendship in the knowledge that I will be able to share it for years to come.

Keith Sutton

Published in 1994 by Osprey, an imprint of Reed Consumer Books Limited, Michelin House, 81 Fulham Road, London SW3 6RB and Auckland, Melbourne, Singapore and Toronto

This book was originally published as
My Ten Years with Ayrton Senna
by Sony Magazines Inc.,
Designed by Takanobu Hatakeyama+Masayuki Shirouzu/
Hot Art Co. Ltd
Design 1994 edition, Behram Kapadia

Photographs and text © Sutton photographic 1994

ISBN 1855325071

Editor Shaun Barrington
Printed and bound by Cayfosa, Barcelona

Ayrton always excelled in the wet: in his first Formula Ford 1600 race at Brands Hatch, at Monaco in 1984 (above right), and for his first F1 victory for Lotus in Portugal (below right), in 1986

FOREWORD

I have known Keith Sutton since I started in circuit racing. We are exactly the same age: our birthdays are only a few days apart, and we have grown up in the sport together. Whether it was Formula 3, Formula 1 or sports cars, Keith has always been there to follow my progress.

When Ayrton Senna came to race in England in 1981, I became aware that he and Keith had become friends and were working together. But the closeness of their relationship didn't prevent Keith taking an interest in my career, of course, not even during that tough but memorable 1983 season when we were fighting for the British F3 title.

Naturally I had noticed Ayrton Senna's meteoric rise through the classic British lower formulas, but I was still somewhat surprised in early 1983 to be constantly asked "Can you beat Senna?" His reputation clearly preceded him, even at that early stage, and as he won the first nine races of that Formula 3 season it was easy to see why.

Then, at Silverstone, I out-qualified him and outraced him in the European F3 round. That weekend, Senna's only weakness was revealed. In his mind it was simply not possible that somebody else using the same equipment could be faster.

There followed a sequence of outrageous races where we crashed, either together or separately. How he failed to break any bones in the accident at Cadwell Park I will never know. He won the championship on the final day. But I think we had done more than enough to impress the right people in Formula 1, because in 1984 we were both competing in the World Championship.

In March this year it was Keith who remembered that Ayrton and I had both graduated to Formula 1 exactly 10 years earlier. At Interlagos he asked us to pose together for his camera. I am of course delighted to have a copy of that photograph to remind me of our rivalry, and of Ayrton.

I can't say I knew him very well on a personal level in those days, but on a professional level I did. Throughout that 1983 season we fought each other hard, but always within the limits. What impressed me at once was his professionalism and commitment.

For such a young man, Senna's sixth sense astounded me. He always knew the correct thing to do. Wet or dry, he knew where the grip was. Was such talent hereditary or was it God-given?

Regardless of the situation, it was obvious from the beginning, from the first moment, that he was something special. He seemed to know by instinct where the limit was - not after the corner, but before. It was as if he was able to anticipate the reaction that would be required: in qualifying, at the start, in traffic or in rain. His was a truly remarkable ability, fully deserving of those three F1 world championships, and more.

Sadly for me, we never did become close friends. Nevertheless, it was certainly a privilege to have known him as a man. I am glad, too, that I experienced his skills from the ultimate grandstand seat: another race car.

Martin Brundle
King's Lynn, Norfolk, England
29th August, 1994

AYRTON SENNA DA SILVA 1960-1994

My interest in photography came about when I was just seventeen. My father was a keen amateur and he lent me his camera. As we had been going to the Oulton Park circuit for so long, the circuit manager gave me a press pass. As soon as I got onto the trackside at Old Hall Corner without any fencing between myself and the racing car, I knew at that precise moment where my true destination lay.

After three years covering motor races around England as a hobby, I turned freelance in 1980 aged twenty. I travelled around Europe and England and covered as many races as I could, but it was a struggle. Then at the start of 1981, luck came my way...

I first saw Ayrton Senna Da Silva at Thruxton circuit In England on March 8th 1981. I was in my second year as a freelance motorsport photographer and I was there working for a Brazilian motorsport magazine who wanted photographs of Brazilian drivers racing in England. I was shy in those days so I never introduced myself to him - I just took lots of photographs of him... in the paddock, on the track - he must have wondered why this photographer whom he had never seen before was taking so many rolls of film of him at only his second race in a racing car! That day he finished third.

For some reason, I decided to go down to Brands Hatch the following weekend on the train, using a free British Rail Promotion Ticket. It was a long way from my home in Cheadle, in fact, it took me eight hours travelling time there and back.

I had just arrived in the paddock when he approached me after recognising me from Thruxton. "Are you a professional photographer?" he enquired. "Yes of course" was my reply. "Well, I need photographs to send to Brazil on a regular basis, can you help me out?" Of course I agreed. That day, he went on to win his heat, then he won the race. It was very exciting and I was there on the podium to capture the moment. It was late evening, the light was fantastic and I took memorable photographs of him with his wife Lilliane. That was the start of my relationship with Ayrton Senna da Silva. I carried on working with him and taking his photographs, writing his press releases, answering his fan mail and handling his pr work for four years.

My closest and most precious memories of Ayrton are the years I was close to him: 1981-84.

We were similar in age, (I was about a year older than him), we both had the same ambitions to succeed, him as a driver and myself as a photographer, and that was to be part of Formula One - the pinnacle of motorsport. We both knew it would take time and as he competed in Formula Ford 1600, Formula Ford 2000 and Formula Three, I photographed him and followed him into Formula One. During 1981 and 1982, he lived in Norfolk close to the two teams he raced for, Van Diemen Racing and Rushen Green Racing. I would often stay at his home which he shared with fellow Brazilian driver Mauricio Gugelmin and his wife Stella. We used to talk about music, movies, girls, ambitions, Brazil, and then sit down to eat one of Stella's speciality Brazilian dishes. In return, Senna used to stay at my home when he was visiting Oulton Park. I had a lot of good times and memories from 1981, but I was put into a state of shock on September 29th when he announced at Brands Hatch that he was retiring from racing because his father needed help on his farm in Brazil and through lack of sponsorship. However, I had a feeling that the real reason was that his wife Lilliane, whom he had married in February, did not like being away from Brazil and became very nervous when he was racing.

Luckily, he returned to the scene in 1982, racing in Formula Ford 2000 for Rushen Green Racing. I suggested to him that we should send photographs and press releases after each race to all the magazines around the world and to the Grand Prix Team Managers, letting them know about Ayrton's performances. Headed notepaper was organised for him with his helmet in all the colour; at the bottom of the paper read 'For further information, contact Keith Sutton, 17 Ashfield Road, Cheadle, Cheshire.' I wasn't a journalist or a writer, I just wanted to help him because I saw the talent and I thought by helping him it would help me.

In 1982, Ayrton competed in both the British and European Formula Ford 2000 championships. I tried to cover as many of his races as possible while trying to cover European Formula Two, British Formula Three and photograph his friend Mauricio Gugelmin in Formula Ford 1600 in England. Fortunately, two of the European Formula Ford 2000 races supported the Grands Prix in Holland and Austria, where he drove to victory in both. The following weekend he was competing in

Denmark, a race which would clinch him the Championship. Whilst in Austria, he asked me if I would like to go to Denmark, he said he would pay the airfare and hotel. I was delighted and I even remember organising the air tickets for him. It was a marvellous weekend which I will never forget. On the return flight to England he told me how he had split up with his wife and had met a Brazilian girl who studied in Brussels, Belgium.

It was also on that flight that he discussed the idea of me being his photographer when he got into Formula One. 1983 saw him graduate to Formula Three and win the championship, after a hard fought battle with Martin Brundle at the final round at Thruxton. That night he asked me to join him, his mother and father and team owner of West Surrey Racing, Mr. Dick Bennetts, and other members of the team for a meal at a restaurant at Shepperton, near to where West Surrey Racing was based. It was a memorable evening, with lots of food and drink and a very late night. To thank me for all the help and all the work I had done for him, he invited me to Brazil for his first Grand Prix in the Toleman. He told me he would take care of the airfare and hotel. I couldn't believe it, I was so happy to go to Brazil, his home and to a country I had always wanted to visit after hearing so much about it from him. I had a great time in Brazil and although I had told him I wasn't prepared to be his personal photographer, he understood my situation and accepted my decision. I had decided that I wanted to be independent and in 1985, I formed Sutton Photographic with my brother Mark. I continued to follow Ayrton's career with a special interest during the following years and I was privileged to be there to see the highs and lows.

The high was undoubtedly when he finally reached his goal, winning the World Championship in 1988. I had never seen him so thrilled, happy and emotional. I remained at the circuit as dusk descended in the Suzuka pit lane, while he watched a replay of the race on the big television screen. My photographs captured the emotion in his eyes as he watched the race and realised he was the World Champion.

Ayrton Senna Da Silva was a unique man. He was one of the most lucid and thoughtful champions the world has ever seen. He was a complex, emotional, passionate, introverted, lonely, mysterious and religious man; driven by an overwhelming desire to do everything to the best of his ability. Behind, or near to the wheel, Senna was cool, calculating and regularly ruthless. But away from the track he was charming, caring and friendly. Most of our conversations over the years since he entered Formula One tended to be at airports. He always used to ask me about how my career and business was going and also how my parents were.

Ayrton Senna is arguably the best racing driver the world has ever seen. His sheer skill and commitment had brought him three world titles and the record of success was only just beginning. He adored his family, respecting his father and idolising his mother. A noticeable trait was that he always had a remarkable knack of putting children totally at ease. I remember when I used to go to Oulton Park to photograph him in 1981, there was a twelve-year-old girl called Cathy Beswick from Stockport who was probably his first fan. She adored him and he always gave his time to her and posed for photographs.

I shall miss Ayrton Senna like millions of people around the world. Formula One has lost a hero and a champion and it will never be the same again.

Keith Sutton

Keith Sutton
Towcester, Northamptonshire, England
4th May, 1994

WINNING FROM THE BEGINNING
1981-84

The Pace British FF2000 champion of 1982

Thruxton circuit, 8th March 1981. Despite the sunshine peering weakly from behind the scudding clouds, it is a cold day. The wind gusts over the tarmac and makes my eyes water as I peer through the viewfinder of my Nikon.

I concentrate on pulling a face into focus. Its owner, less than five metres in front of me, wears a red fire suit with a small Brazilian flag on the breast. No other identification. The face is handsome and the eyes record everything that is happening. In years to come, these strong, memorable features will become familiar to millions, staring out of advertisements, from under headlines and on TV.

Thirteen years later, I can confess that I needed to capture the image on my precious film only because it had been commissioned by a Brazilian magazine. My pictures would buy a few litres of fuel for my car, a few more rolls of film, food and rent to survive until the next race. Ambition is the foundation of a career, whether you're a photographer or a sportsman. At the beginning, my own sights were not set high. While this was my second season as a racing photographer, I would soon discover that Ayrton Senna da Silva – the driver in my pictures – was already a high achiever. Finishing 2nd or 3rd held no pleasure for him. He wanted to win.

There were things that we had in common, though. At Thruxton we had not spoken, but one week later, at Brands Hatch, we met again – and chatted. He was not yet 20, one year younger than me, yet he was already business-minded.

Was I interested in selling him some personal photos for him to send home, to sponsors and for the press? Of course. Two professional careers in racing started that day. Ayrton's when he won what was his third ever car race in heavy rain, the most difficult of conditions. Mine when I eagerly agreed to supply him with the pictures he needed.

In the next four years, Ayrton Senna went further and faster than any driver I have known. Nothing would stop him. In 1981, he won two national British titles in Formula Ford 1600. In 1982, he cleaned up in the British and European Formula Ford 2000 series. In 1983 he did the same in the British Formula 3 championship. A year later he was in Formula 1 with Toleman, the team which later became Benetton Formula. Thanks to him, perhaps inspired by him, I too have made a little progress. Even before we met, I was already covering Formula 1. All I needed to become one of hundreds of photographers was a camera, an eye for a good picture and a press pass. What he needed to become

one of the 26 men on the grid was talent. And Senna's talent was so huge, so impossible to ignore, that by the end of 1983 he had been invited to test cars belonging not just to Toleman but to Williams, McLaren and Brabham, too.

From a flood of memories, four episodes particularly epitomise Ayrton Senna for me during those first four years. One was the Brands Hatch race, his first win in a racing car, which I was able to share. By 1982 I had been officially appointed as his press officer and he paid for me to join him at the deciding round of the European Formula Ford 2000 championships, at the Jyllandsring in Denmark. .Although Ayrton paid all the expenses, we had to share a hotel room. I was happy – especially when he won the race and the championship. That night we celebrated with a meal followed by a few drinks in a local nightclub.

The next time we celebrated a championship was in October 1983. It was the evening after Ayrton had clinched the British Formula 3 title at Thruxton, a race which brilliantly demonstrated the combination of technical aptitude and daring which made him almost unbeatable in all forms of racing. His opponent that year had been Martin Brundle, the tough and intelligent British driver who was later to become a world champion in sports car racing and who is now of course still competing in F1. After a slow start to the season, Brundle and his entrant, Eddie Jordan, found some extra power. It was sufficient to surprise Senna and put Brundle into contention for the title.

In this last race, though, Senna and his team chief, F3 veteran Dick Bennetts, had a trick up their sleeves. It was a cold day, and to ensure that the oil temperature of his Ralt's engine reached operating temperature as quickly as possible, Senna planned to start the race with the oil cooler taped over. On the second or third lap, he would have to loosen his seat belts – something which he had already practised – and lean out of the cockpit to rip away the tape. He was in the lead, but only by a few fractions of a second, when a soaring oil temperature reading told him he would have to rip away the tape immediately. Somehow he managed to do it whilst braking for the chicane. Brundle, in third place, saw it happening – and knew instantly that he was beaten.

On the podium, Senna was ecstatic. His father, Milton da Silva, was there, with Ayrton's mother. For me, it was yet another insight into Ayrton Senna. The strength of his family's love and support transcended all other relationships in his life.

A new cap. Halfway through the 1984 season, Toleman switched from Pirelli to Michelin tyres. The dispute left the team without tyres in 1985 – but Ayrton had already signed with Lotus

Under perfect control - like most things that Ayrton attempted

The last of these four abiding memories dates back to July 1983. It was two days after the British Grand Prix, and Ayrton had been invited by Frank Williams to try one of his F1 cars. Although Williams' was a top team (his driver Keke Rosberg had been world champion in 1982), the new Honda turbo V6 was not yet ready to race, and the cars were still using Ford-Cosworth V8 power.

The ever-approachable Frank had offered advice which Ayrton had willingly accepted. And when the test drive was offered, he did not hesitate to accept. As Ayrton was to tell me, he had waited seven years, since his first kart race, for this day. For the rest of his career he felt a special debt of gratitude to Frank Williams for being the first F1 team boss to show faith in his ability and they would join forces several years on..

Though anxious to get started, he took his time about getting comfortable in the car. He checked the instruments and switches and asked about the wings and their settings. Only then did he set off to begin the greatest adventure of his life. Looking back, he was more than satisfied. "I didn't spin, I sweated a lot ... and Frank Williams was pleased with me," he said. Armed with this experience, he was confident that he could make the jump from Formula 3 to Formula 1 and in 1984, with the Toleman team, that is what precisely what he did. He was on his way...

The choice of Toleman as his first F1 team was entirely Ayrton's. It surprised me at the time, because he also had offers from McLaren and Williams. But Ayrton had figured out exactly what he wanted from a team in his first season of F1, and Toleman was the perfect choice. He used the Hart turbo engine and had a tyre contract with Pirelli. These items required development — which guaranteed plenty of test driving for the new driver. At the same time, the pressure on him to win would not be great, because no one expected Toleman to beat big names like McLaren-TAG or Williams-Honda.

Whilst at Toleman, the full extent of Ayrton's technical knowledge became apparent, particularly in his relations with the Pirelli technicians. His first test, after signing with Toleman, took place in Rio in February 1984. The weather in Brazil was almost intolerably hot, and Ayrton had not yet developed the physical stamina required for F1 racing. But the Pirelli technicians were amazed to learn so much about the performance of their tyres from a man who had probably covered less than 500 kms in an F1 car. In fact, Ayrton demanded changes to the structure and flexibility of the tyres, as though he had been using them for years.

I did not attend that test, but thanks to Ayrton's generosity, I was present for his first Grand Prix at that same Rio circuit on March 25. Although the car failed, Ayrton did not. In his very first car race in his home country, he showed speed and consistency. Two weeks later in South Africa, he scored one point for sixth place in only his second GP. In the first race of the European season, in Belgium, he scored yet another point.

Then, in pouring rain at Monaco, Ayrton very nearly became the first man to win a Grand Prix for Toleman, and for Pirelli, whose tyres had not won in F1 since 1957. Halfway through the race, just as he was closing on the leader, Alain Prost, the race was stopped. Prost, who had already decided to pull into the pits, crossed the finishing line at walking speed. Only a few metres after passing the line, the Toleman went past the McLaren. Understandably, Ayrton was furious. The race had been allowed to start because TV stations around the world expected it. In fact the rain had fallen harder at the start of the 1984 Monaco GP than at the finish. If it was too dangerous when the race was stopped, then why was it ever allowed to start? These and other questions about the race continue to be discussed today. Ayrton would have to wait another year for his first F1 victory.

At home using the pool, and hobby flying his radio-controlled helicopter in Esher, near London, with fellow-Brazilian and long-time friend Mauricio Gugelmin. In 1984, Ayrton followed an exercise program set for him by the coach of Brazil's national volleyball team

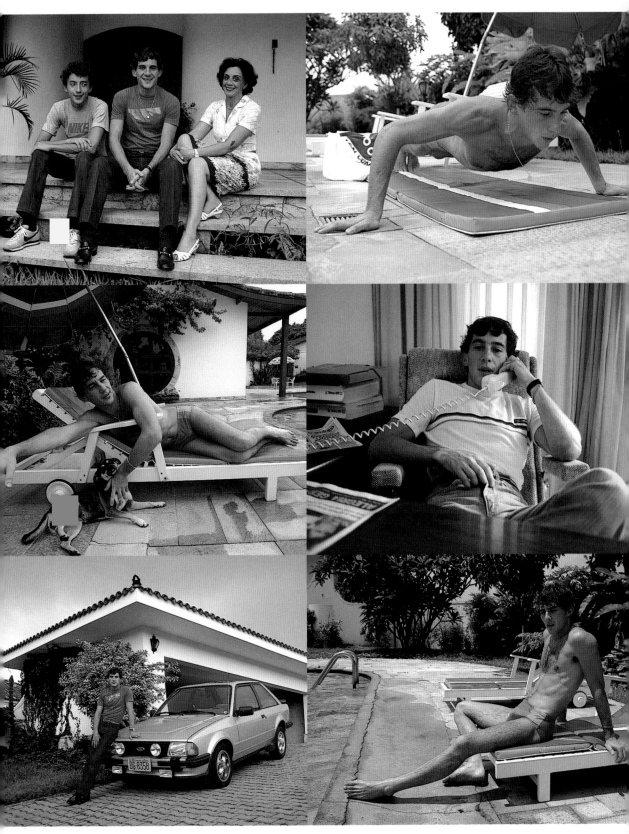

Top left At the front door relaxing with the family. Father Milton da Silva was absent on business when these photographs were taken, at the family farm in the interior

Top right Despite his daily press-ups, it would take several races before Ayrton acquired the stamina to keep him going strongly for a full FI race distance

Bottom left Ford was the first company to offer a courtesy car – Sao Paulo, 1984

Ayrton would become fitter to withstand the rigours of F1; the days when a driver could put down his gin and tonic, put on his goggles and drive are long gone, as the exercise regimes today of drivers such as Michael Schumacher indicate

June 21, Silverstone. Ayrton's mechanic Malcolm Pudden watches carefully as the works Van Diemen Formula Ford team prepares to do battle

Waiting for his race, the young Formula Ford driver shows the same concentration and determination which was to become familiar in Formula 1

March 15, 1981, Brands Hatch: and Ayrton's first win in Formula Ford. I had to persuade the commentator to let me use his box to shoot the start. Ayrton (31) is already in front

At the notorious Mallory Park race, Mansilla (8) never expected his new team-mate — with only three races behind him — to get as close to him as this, (below right) so when Ayrton attacked, Mansilla 'closed the door' and put him off the road. A furious Ayrton had to make do with second place ...

... while Mansilla gets the cheers of the crowd on his victory lap (top left). The 1981 clash with Enrique Mansilla ended in body damage for Ayrton's car; you could never say that Ayrton was that strange, English invention, a good loser

Ayrton thinks he has won at Silverstone in June 1981, but was in fact beaten into 2nd place by Rick Morris who had jumped the chicane. His only consolation was to claim a handsome victory in the qualifying heat

Top Left A big kiss from Liliane after winning at Oulton. Although she knew nothing about racing, I am sure that her loyalty and companionship eased her husband's difficulties in being alone in a strange land

Top right and centre left The clash at Mallory Park. Enrique Mansilla had just collected the trophy when an angry Brazilian takes him by the neck. The restraining hand on Ayrton's shoulder belongs to his mechanic, Malcolm "Puddy" Pullen. Mansilla was quite shocked

Centre right With Alfonso 'Alfie' Toledano, the Mexican driver who helped and befriended Ayrton during his first season with the Van Diemen team

Bottom left My best customer looks satisfied with my first work for him: photos of him being congratulated by Liliane after his very first FF victory

Bottom right Liliane gives her husband a special smile. They had been married for only one month

Winning at Brands Hatch in March 1981. By now Ayrton's extraordinarily good technical feedback had persuaded Van Diemen boss Ralph Firman that he was the best driver on the team, despite the superior experience of team-mates Mansilla and Toledano

Waiting to go on to the track. The set of the face and the stern eyes show that Ayrton is totally concentrated on the job which he is about to do. Practice or race, it was always a serious moment for him

At the end of 1981, Ayrton unexpectedly went home to Brazil at the request of his father – and to get divorced. When he returned to England, the best drive he could find was with the private Formula Ford 2000 team of Dennis Rushen

AYRTON SENNA

The cockpit of the Van Diemen RF82 from which two championships – one British, the other European – were won by far and away 1982's most successful Formula Ford 2000 driver

It is difficult to believe that the mature face in my picture belonged to a man who was still only 21 years old. Some found it strange in 1982 when Ayrton decided to abandon his father's family name (da Silva) in favour of 'Senna', his mother's family name. In fact, this is common practice in most South American countries

Illustrating the importance of technique at Mallory Park: in a category of racing as competitive as Formula Ford 2000, time can be saved by hugging the inside of a hairpin. No one got closer than this!

Jyllandsring, Denmark, August 1982. I formed a close friendship with Dennis Rushen, who respected Ayrton's abilities and concentrated on organising the team for him as efficiently as possible

Donington (below) and Oulton Park (below right). After only ten races in Formula Ford, Ayrton had perfected his famous fast-starting technique, designed to leave rivals gasping by the end of the first lap. Of the 28 races which he contested in 1982 with the Rushen Green FF2000 Van Diemen RF82, he won 22

The Euro-final at Jyllandsring in Denmark (top) saw Ayrton way out in front, as for most of the 1982 Formula Ford 2000 season

Head down and arms up: the moment of triumph at Jyllandsring as Ayrton savours victory in the 1982 European Formula Ford 2000 championship

Bottom left Being congratulated by F1 team boss Emerson Fittipaldi after winning the FF2000 race which supported the 1982 Austrian GP. It was Fittipaldi driver Chico Serra (centre) who brought Ayrton to England for his first racing car test in November 1980

Centre left Celebrating in Denmark. As the winning team at Jyllandsring, the Rushen Green crew seem to have made a few friends. That's me on the far right

Bottom right There were not many occasions when I saw Ayrton take a drink, but the evening when he won the European Formula Ford 2000 championship was an exception

Posing happily as the double Champion for 1982

The concentration of a champion

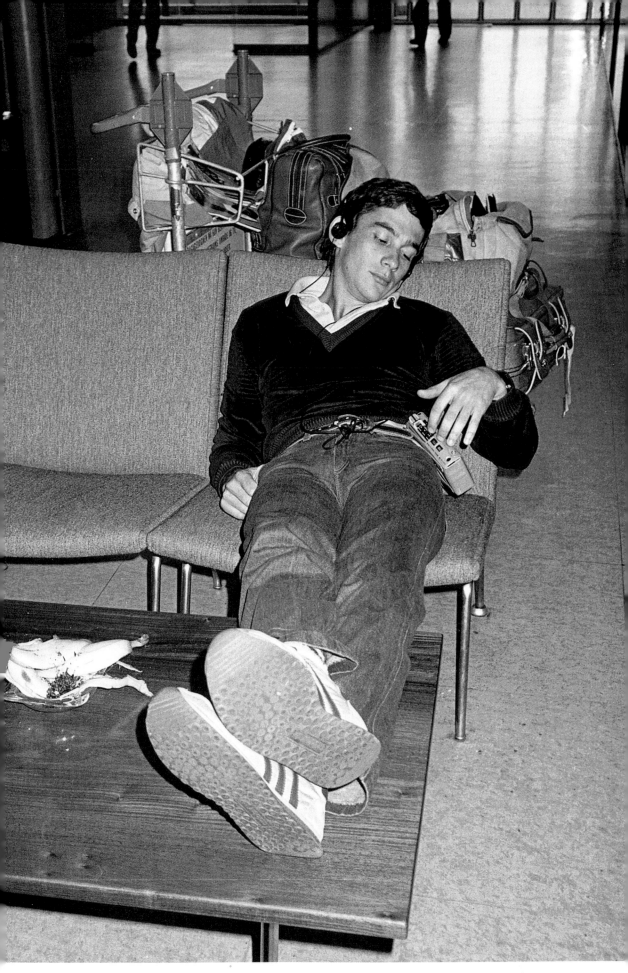

Off duty. Copenhagen airport, August 1982. With his first important international success behind him, the new European Formula Ford 2000 champion finds time to relax

A last minute check as Ayrton waits, helmet off as usual, for the signal to take his West Surrey Racing Ralt on to the track for another round of the 1983 British Formula 3 championship

Cadwell Park, June 1983. Although he has already taken pole position, with five minutes of qualifying left, Ayrton tries to better his time. It proved to be a serious mistake ...

There is nothing immediately glamorous, and certainly nothing warm, about an early season round of the British F3 championship, as this friend of Ayrton discovered in April 1983

In a big accident, the West Surrey Ralt is destroyed during qualifying at Cadwell. A driving mistake sends the car wide and it hits a marshals' post. After 10 races without damage to his car, Dick Bennetts of West Surrey Racing had cancelled the insurance only a few days earlier ...

Lining up in the paddock at Thruxton, May 1983. Behind wait Englishman Martin Brundle and American Davy Jones, who would both later race Jaguar sports cars

Top In 1983, nothing distracted the new Formula 3 racing sensation, not even Christine, the Brazilian girlfriend
Bottom While his Brazilian driver went straight from F3 success to F1, team chief Dick Bennetts chose to stay in the formula, where he continued the search for future world champions

Battling with Martin Brundle in the British Formula Three Championship

Top A publicity shot for the F3 Ralt-Toyota, which I learned later had been published by newspapers all over Brazil
Bottom Accelerating away from the line at Thruxton in May 1983, for once it is Martin Brundle who has a slight advantage. Ayrton won the race, though

Top left Trying to stay calm at Mallory Park as the Rushen Green mechanics change an engine before the race starts. The winner, of course, was the Brazilian in dark glasses

Centre left Martin Brundle (left) looked less than delighted with 2nd place behind his rival at Thruxton in March. By the end of the season, though, he had come close to catching up the Brazilian's points advantage. Both Martin and Allen Berg take avoiding action (bottom right) at another victory celebration

Centre right Another pre-race drama as Dick Bennetts of West Surrey Racing helps his mechanics to solve a last-minute hitch. Look who is the calmest person in the picture

Looking perplexed with the laurels at Donington Park in March 1983. Look at the number of sponsors' names creeping on to the overalls

Posing happily for me with the first laurel wreath

By the middle of the summer of 1983, a Senna Fan Club was being formed. But their idol did not need any help to tell him which way he was going: he was heading for F1

Top left and centre right Third race in Formula Ford: celebrating the first win with wife Liliane. Team mate Alfredo Toledano shares the happiness

Bottom left September 1981 and Ayrton's final race in Formula Ford 1600: after finishing 2nd to Rick Morris (wearing laurels), he returned unexpectedly to Brazil

The Van Diemen was Ayrton's first racing car. He felt much less comfortable in it than he did with his go-karts

Van Diemen's excellent FF2000, basically a regular FF1600 car using wings and slick tyres, was used for the British and European championships – and won both

One of the publicity shots which we took in order to encourage potential sponsors

The 1982 season, in FF2000, brought more success – so far no sponsorship however, which in the end, of course, would be vital if Ayrton's career was not to be brilliant but shortlived

Winning at Oulton Park in FF2000; victory throughout the season came almost as a matter of course

Another FF2000 win – the opposition (background) fell over each other trying to catch up

The West Surrey mechanics give the Ralt-Toyota a last check on the grid

Domination: the first nine races in F3 with the West Surrey team's Ralt-Toyota produced nine wins

With the move up to Formula 3 in 1983, the sponsorship is finally on tap

A publicity shot taken from the back of an estate car. We're not really keeping up with the F3 car at full throttle: I used a slow shutter speed to turn 30 mph into 90!

Looking pensive, now with Toleman, 1984

Yet another F3 podium gathering with Britain's Martin Brundle (right) and Canadian Allen Berg

Winning at Macau in 1983 was very important to Ayrton, beating the best drivers in Europe. He declined to race in the F3 Monaco event that year, feeling that the lack of regulations regarding tyres meant lack of parity, and the driver with the best rubber (Michelin) would inevitably win. Yokohamas for all at Macau. Ayrton arrived jet lagged after testing the Brabham in France, having never seen the circuit before, and promptly took pole position and the honours. Hong Kong businessman Teddy Yip (top left) was Theodores racing team owner

Ayrton's only appearance in a Group C sports car, at Nurburgring in 1984. Sharing this Joest Porsche 956 with Stefan Johansson and Henri Pescarolo, he finished 8th. Joest mechanics (below) refuel the Porsche

Top left Carefully checking the Williams's tyres during the Donington test

Top right Ayrton tells the owner about his reactions to the Fl Williams-Cosworth during the test

Frank Williams told Ayrton that he did not have a place for him on his team in 1984 – it was ten years before they joined forces

The Toleman-Hart turbo in Rio, 1984. Ayrton chose to drive for this team because he knew there would be no pressure on him to win immediately

Top left Sergio Tacchini, an Italian brand of sports clothing, was one of Toleman's sponsors in 1984

Top right Brands Hatch, 1984. On his way to 3rd place at a circuit which he knew well from junior racing days

Bottom left Prince Michael of Kent, cousin to Her Majesty Queen Elizabeth, presents the trophy to McLaren's Ron Dennis for Lauda's 1984 British victory. Ron had already tried to sign Ayrton, without success

First Fl race, with Toleman, in March 1984. The deal with Marlboro was done only two days earlier

GETTING ESTABLISHED IN F1
1985-87

Business in Brazil. Outside his Sao Paulo office with Armando Teixeira, family friend and personal manager

Almost as soon as Ayrton Senna and I became friends, I discovered how important go-kart racing had been – and still was – in his life. I now believe that this form of motorsport had been responsible for his ambitions, even forming his character. Ever since he was four years old, all his energy had been devoted to practising motor sport. As his friend Mauricio Gugelmin has said, karting in Brazil at that time was a true sport, with equal equipment for everyone and a wonderful spirit of camaraderie.

The constant exposure to engines, tyres and chassis had left Ayrton with very little room for other ambitions. He told me that he had completed his schooling under threat from his father that the privilege of going to the track would be withdrawn if he did not study. Ayrton did not talk about graduation. Instead, he spoke about the day at Interlagos – July 1, 1973 – when he was considered old enough to enter a kart race – which he won.

Throughout 1981 and 1982 he even tried to combine kart racing with his car career by competing in the kart world championships. He failed because his equipment was not fully competitive. The frustration of those two failures stayed with him, I believe, until he won the F1 championship for the first time, in 1988. Karting, Ayrton once said, was the only "pure" form of racing which he knew.

When he came to England with his friend Chico Serra at the end of 1980, to try a Formula Ford car, he discovered that he did not enjoy the physical feeling of driving a racing car. The reactions of the comparatively low-powered Formula Ford and Formula 3 cars which he raced for three years felt slower than the go-karts which he had loved to take to the limit. He did not rediscover that feeling until he arrived in Formula 1, with Toleman, in 1984.

The experience with Toleman had been excellent. He learned quickly, and before the end of the year had finished three times on the podium. Very few drivers have achieved as much in their first season of F1 racing. As the season went on, Ayrton told me, he realised that there was nothing magic about a Formula 1 car. The most important thing, he said, was to be in the right team in the right year.

Inevitably, other team managers wanted to discuss his future with him. In the long term interests of his career, Ayrton decided that a change of team would be the correct move. In August, with six races still to be contested in the 1984 championship, Team Lotus issued a press release to announce that Ayrton Senna had signed a three-year contract. The news shocked Toleman, whose manager also issued a press

release to point out that there was a contract between the team and its driver, which would be enforced.

In reality, the situation was not as simple as that: Ayrton had the right to buy his release from his obligations to Toleman. Unfortunately, the press release from Lotus was the first notification to Toleman that he wanted to exercise that right. "It was a pity," Ayrton told me: "I made the announcement as soon as possible, to give Toleman an opportunity to find a replacement for me. That was my intention."

The incident soured Toleman's attitude to Ayrton, who found himself the object of various legal moves. Before these were settled, he was "suspended" by the team from taking part in the Italian GP, an incident which upset him so much that it made him physically ill.

Yet it also stiffened his resolution to do well. At the Portuguese GP, with the help of some engine improvements, the Toleman was superior to any car on the track except the two McLarens with their TAG-Porsche engines. It was the last race of the season, and for the third time that year Ayrton finished the day on the podium.

When Ayrton joined Lotus, this famous British team was still regarded as a front-runner. But Ayrton, just as he had done with Toleman, knew how to use the reputation and resources of Lotus to gain the maximum prestige for himself. With the benefit of hindsight, it was an excellent decision by Lotus to engage such a gifted driver. Ayrton's first victory with the team, in the rain at Estoril (Portugal) in April 1985, was not only memorable for him, it was also a landmark for Lotus, who had struggled on without a victory since August 1982.

The start of his association with Lotus was marked by a rare bout of ill health. At the beginning of December, while he was still in Europe, Ayrton suffered an attack of Bell's Palsy, a viral infection which paralysed the right side of his face. Professor Watkins, the British neurologist who heads the FISA medical team at F1 races, put Ayrton under medication.

Back home in Brazil, Ayrton had a relapse. This was serious. Professor Watkins gloomily informed him that driving was out of the question, partly because the right eye would not focus, but also because the medication was too strong to make driving under its influence safe.

Instead of taking part in the two winter test sessions planned by Lotus at Ricard and Daytona, Ayrton was obliged to stay at home while his new team mate, the Italian Elio de Angelis, got on with the demanding work of developing the car.

When JPS withdrew from F1 at the end of 1986, Lotus pulled off a big deal with Camel. It was Ayrton's first experience with a multinational sponsor – and he took his responsibilities seriously

In the circumstances, Ayrton was understandably apprehensive about the start of his association with Lotus. He had never worked with the car's designer Gerard Ducarouge before. He had no experience with the Renault V6 turbo engine either, or with the Goodyear tyres used by Lotus. However, after one test session and one race (in Brazil, where he stopped with electrical trouble), Senna was a winner with Lotus. It happened in Portugal, yet again under the most difficult of conditions. In pouring rain, he led from start to finish. "I had several bad moments," he told me, "and the worst was when I went with all four wheels off the road. The car just hit a big puddle and went straight out of the track. Fortunately it didn't hit anything..."

This first F1 victory was full of significance for Ayrton. It gave the team full confidence in him, and gave him a psychological advantage over De Angelis, who was to leave at the end of the year. Yet again, the way was open for Ayrton to dominate his chosen team.

In his three years with Lotus, Ayrton won a total of six GPs. Yet as he became more successful, his demands would hurt the team. An example was his refusal to have the talented British driver Derek Warwick as his team mate in 1986, which annoyed the British press. He also persuaded Lotus to switch from Renault to Honda engines in 1987, thus breaking the contract which the team had signed with the French company.

When the time came, Ayrton knew that his next career move would be to the team which would give him the world championship. By 1987, it was clear that Lotus was not that team. In September 1987, it was announced that he would join McLaren in 1988, in effect taking Honda with him. As a courtesy, Lotus was allowed to keep the Honda turbo. But Honda ended the association at the end of 1988, and from that point onwards the team declined. In his three years at Lotus, Ayrton had learned to take advantage of situations not just on the race track but also within a team. He had become a great manipulator. And although no one knew it yet, his next victim would be the Frenchman who was comfortably established at McLaren...

Estoril, 1985. The first GP win in treacherous conditions. Forty more GP victories would follow

Lifting a wheel in Australia in 1986. By then Renault had withdrawn its own F1 team and Lotus carried the hopes of the French company, which withdrew its support (and its powerful V6 engine) from Grand Prix racing altogether at the end of the year, leaving the way clear for a Lotus-Honda alliance in 1987

Throughout 1986, Ayrton cajoled and inspired Lotus and Renault to give him the best equipment. However, Williams and Honda were invariably superior

The serious face goes on as Ayrton prepares to qualify. It was Lotus designer Gerard Ducarouge who gave him the nickname 'Magic'

Although Lotus was still a top team when Ayrton joined in 1985, it was probably his genius and inspiration which lifted the team and kept it winning throughout 1986 and then 1987. Lotus has certainly not been the same since he left

Under brakes for the Loews hairpin, Ayrton takes the JPS Lotus-Renault to 3rd place at Monaco in 1986

Centre left With three races to go of the 1986 season, four drivers had a chance of being champion: Ayrton (far left), Alain Prost, Nigel Mansell and Nelson Piquet. Prost finally took it, but only after the Williams team had virtually made a gift of it to him
Centre right Happy with third place at the 1985 Dutch GP
Bottom left 'Go flat out Ayrton' urge the JPS posters in Brazil, 1985

Top left French Grand Prix, 1986
Top right Detroit, 1986. The Lotus crew salutes Ayrton's fourth F1 victory
Bottom left The Lotus hits one of the bumps and sends up sparks at Spa Francorchamps during the 1986 Belgian Grand Prix
Bottom right A section of the huge crowd at the 1986 Brazilian GP in Rio

Waiting for help at Estoril in 1985 after a mechanical failure in practice

Top Leading from Alain Prost in 1985, a future team mate and intense rival
Bottom Monaco 1986. Third place behind the McLarens of Alain Prost and Keke Rosberg

Brazil, 1987: a new season, a new engine (Honda turbo) and a new team-mate in Satoru Nakajima

An isolated figure inside the Lotus-Honda truck; thoughts, no doubt, of the treacherous road to the Formula 1 Championship

The 1987 season saw Lotus' pioneering work with computer-controlled 'active' suspension – since banned due to its expense and complexity. Ayrton was intensely involved in the development of the 'springless' suspension and won both of the team's GP successes, at Monaco and Detroit

France, 1987. The comfortable computer-controlled 'active ride' suspension of the Lotus-Honda played an important part in the first of Ayrton's two wins of the season

Though the 'active' Lotus-Honda was effective on slower street-type circuits, it suffered on high-speed tracks. Not even a switch to 'lo-line' bodywork inspired by the Williams improved the situation

Braking late in England, 1987, with the discs going for the burn

Top left Lotus's computer-controlled suspension made the 1987 Monaco GP almost too easy: Ayrton won without strain and said he could have gone a full race distance all over again
Centre left With Satoru Nakajima, 1987 team mate
Bottom right Hockenheim 1987. Talking business with race engineer Steve Hallam, who followed Ayrton to McLaren in 1991

Lotus-Honda days: trying to figure out how to beat Williams who had the same engine. The two victories at Monaco and Detroit in 1987 were arguably insufficient reward for the work which Ayrton did with Lotus

First time out in public for the 1987 Lotus-Honda and Camel had been in Brazil, in the welcoming sunshine of Rio's Jacarepagua circuit. The season promised much, but delivered little

Japanese fans (top), Detroit fans (bottom), and the Brazilian fans in Portugal, 1989, proclaim their origins in the state of Ceara; followers just about everywhere

FROM PRINCE TO KING:
SENNA RULES THE WORLD
1988-93

The flags and banners followed Senna throughout his career. Not all of the fans could spell, ('Aylton' was an endearing Japanese error) – and on occasion the Italian fans took the opportunity to insult the Federation

Monza, September 5, 1987. In the heat of a late summer's afternoon in Italy, a formal announcement is made; that Ayrton Senna has been recruited by McLaren for 1988. Honda decides to stay with Ayrton, therefore switching its support from Williams to McLaren. The low sun makes excellent conditions for photography, and my pictures show everyone involved looking a little uncomfortable.

Both Ayrton and Alain are nervous. But while Prost frowns constantly, I can see confidence on Ayrton's face. His arrival at McLaren, with Honda as part of the deal, has created the strongest team in racing. Although they are to be "co-number one" drivers, Prost is unquestionably the superior, with his four years at McLaren already behind him. But however friendly the Frenchman might have become with McLaren chief Ron Dennis, Senna is now a threat to Prost's supremacy.

At Monza and afterwards, Dennis emphasised his team's ability to provide both drivers with identical equipment. He spoke confidently of their "maturity" and their willingness to observe McLaren's "discipline." Looking back, it was all hopelessly optimistic. In 1987, Dennis himself had scoffed at Frank Williams' inability to keep the peace between Piquet and Mansell. The McLaren chief would have far more serious strife in his own team, ending only with the departure of Prost after two years. When you put two lions in a cage, you do not expect them to cuddle up every night.

While fighting each other for the world championship, the two McLaren men would have to share information and intelligence. The importance of this would not become clear for several months, because Ayrton spent much of the winter at home in Brazil. He would insist on his right to get away from racing for two or three months during the European winter. But as a driver who had been identified with the yellow of Camel, this year he also needed to be out of the public eye for the sake of his new sponsor, Philip Morris/Marlboro.

Inevitably, Prost would criticise Senna for taking such a long winter break and leaving him to do virtually all of the winter testing. This year, though, it gave the Frenchman an opportunity to meet the Honda people, test their engine and discover how they worked.

Ayrton's move to McLaren confirmed to me yet again his ability to make decisions logically, without emotion, using only his extraordinary powers of common sense. Back in the days when I had prepared his press releases, he always particularly insisted that we send a copy to Dr Gozzi, the personal assistant to Mr Ferrari

himself. I sensed then that Ayrton wanted to become a Ferrari driver one day...

Meanwhile at McLaren, it did not take long for Ayrton to strike up good relations with the technicians. And the 1988 season was to be the one when the red and white cars broke all records: 15 victories from 16 starts, and eight of them for Ayrton. However, his first race with McLaren-Honda would be an anticlimax: he had a gearbox problem on the parade lap in Rio, and was disqualified on a technicality after the start was aborted and had to take the team's spare. But even though Prost went on to win, Ayrton had served notice on the Frenchman that his days as McLaren's undisputed number one driver were over.

In one area – pole positions – Ayrton beat Prost handsomely that year. He collected 13 'poles' from 16 races, breaking the old record of nine poles in one season. At the second race of the season, at Imola, he also won the first of that season's eight Senna victories. Ironically, each success created a minor aggravation for the staff at the McLaren factory over the contentious matter of trophies.

Ever since I met him, Ayrton had regarded trophies as essential mementoes. No matter how small or insignificant, they were always carefully packed up and sent back home, at first to the new house which he had bought at Esher, later to Monaco and eventually to Sao Paulo. But McLaren had a long-established tradition that all trophies belong to the team, to be displayed in the "long room" which adjoins the entry hall of the factory at Woking, Berkshire. It was Ayrton who eventually found the solution: he arranged for the makers of all the trophies he won to be traced. They would then be asked to make an exact replica for him to keep.

My memories of that 1988 season are a red and white blur of victories mounting up, and the closeness of Ayrton and Prost as they surged to more and more wins. Ron Dennis was determined to ensure that they had equally good machinery with which to race, and he succeeded. They were only three points apart (Ayrton 75, Prost 72) when they went to Portugal for the 13th race of the season.

This was the final year of the turbo, and the strict limit of 150 litres for fuel obliged the leading drivers to watch their fuel gauges even more keenly than their rear view mirrors. Knowing that Prost was just as concerned about fuel as he was, Ayrton did not expect the challenge which came from the Frenchman on the second lap. As Prost drew alongside him on the pits straight, Ayrton allowed his car to move right, forcing Prost to brush the pit wall at close to

300 km/h. The mechanics in the March pit snatched their signalling boards out of the way and ducked behind the wall, half-expecting Prost to smash into it.

Even though Prost won that day, he was furious afterwards. He felt that his life had been threatened by his team-mate. Nor did his victory – and another in Spain a week later – give him the comfort of consolidating his lead in the world championship. In fact, the points-scoring system (counting only the season's 11 best results) favoured Ayrton's "win or bust" style over Prost's more consistent habit of building up points for lesser placings. The next race, round 15, in Japan, was Ayrton's eighth win. It was just enough to ensure the title for him. Prost played the perfect sportsman at the time, declining to complain about the apparent injustice of a man with 96 points having to take second place to one with 88. In later years, though, he would speak bitterly about the title which was taken from him by the rules.

To Ayrton, as always, there were no doubts at all about the validity of his title. It was the summit of his career, achieved in front of the Japanese fans whose support meant so much to him. He spent that evening in the McLaren pit, watching re-runs of the race on the TV screen and giving interviews to Brazilian journalists. I was one of only two or three photographers who had not disappeared, and I was able to share at least a fraction of the champion's satisfaction. My photographs show the emotion, and a few tears on his face as we enjoyed the crisp evening air at Suzuka. Ayrton often spoke of that day in public. Now, I realise that he saw it as his appointment with destiny. In one interview, published in Brazil, he even spoke of having seen a heavenly vision during the race. His first world championship, he always said, would be the best; the most satisfying and the most memorable.

In the next two years, the Japanese circuit would be the scene of two ugly incidents involving Ayrton and Alain Prost. In name at least, they were still team mates in 1989, when they collided while Ayrton was trying to take the lead. In reality, the two men were no longer even on speaking terms.

The disintegration of their relationship had started with the wheel-banging at Estoril in 1988. Though they were cool towards each other, the two men were still talking at the beginning of 1989. After an incident at Imola in April 1989, however, a wall went up between them. In an attempt to avoid first-lap collisions, they had mutually (but privately) reached a "no passing" agreement for the San Marino GP. The

terms of the agreement were simple: in the first corner they would hold station, without attempting to pass each other. However, immediately after the start at Imola, Senna did not hesitate to use the slipstream of Prost's faster-starting car to dash past, grab the lead and lay the foundations for an important victory in which Prost finished a disillusioned second.

The Frenchman was so furious that he dashed away from the circuit without speaking to anyone. either on the team or in the press. If this was meant to leave Ayrton examining his conscience, it failed. Prost was dismissed as "cracked in the head." As Ayrton painstakingly explained, he had not broken the agreement because he did not regard the place where he had passed his team mate as a corner at all, but merely "part of the straight." In fact, for most of us this 200 mph swerve would most certainly be a corner. In Ayrton's mind, however, it was not – evidently because it requires no real skill or exertion and can be taken flat out by a top F1 driver. Its name is Tamburello.

From that day onwards, Prost and Ayrton might have been in different teams. They spoke to each other only through their engineers. The friendship between Prost and Ron Dennis, which dated back to 1984, just trickled away. It reached rock bottom at Suzuka, where Prost subtly but deliberately nerfed his rival off the track as they braked for the tight chicane.

No matter that Ayrton was completing a daring but legitimate manoeuvre which he had been calculating for many laps. On this day, Prost had the FIA and resident Balestre on his side. Even though Ayrton recovered from the clash and continued, eventually crossing the line in first place, he was excluded from the results. Ron Dennis made a big fuss at the time, holding press conferences in London and Adelaide at which he was able to demonstrate that Ayrton's actions had not transgressed any rules. Yet there was no arguing that Prost had won the title. In spite of assurances that Ayrton's case "would not be allowed to be swept under the carpet", McLaren soon abandoned it.

After the humiliations of their second season together, and long before he secured the 1989 title, Prost renewed his alliance with former McLaren designer John Barnard by joining Ferrari. In 1989 Barnard's elegant design had already proved itself in Nigel Mansell's hands. Prost quickly made himself at home, won five GPs and went to Suzuka with a good chance of beating Ayrton to the title.

Who could forget the tension that built up before the start in Japan, or the dismay when Prost was struck violently from behind at the first corner by Ayrton's McLaren-Honda! I remember the feeling of disappointment that I had for the cessation, after only 400 metres of racing, of the championship duel which millions of people – 200,000 of them in the stands at Suzuka alone – had anticipated so keenly in the weeks before the race.

These two celebrated incidents at Suzuka both settled world championships: to Prost in 1989, and to Ayrton a year later. The circumstances have been analysed by sports writers of every nation. I do not intend to judge them myself, yet I know that there was an element of revenge in the 1990 clash for what had happened in 1989. It took Ayrton two years to admit publicly that he had no intention of allowing Prost to reach the first corner ahead of him. Inside F1, though, everyone knew that it had been deliberate.

Perhaps we should not be surprised that such things can happen. With so much at stake, from both sporting and financial standpoints, Formula I has become a global business. Winning is everything. In the first ten years of my own involvement with Grand Prix racing, the budget required to run a top team increased by perhaps ten times, and the rewards for the drivers by an even greater factor.

These elements have not had a beneficial effect on the sporting side of F1. Indeed, modern racing has become a corporate activity, with financial and technical decisions made at boardroom level. Twenty-five years ago, the basic design of a successful F1 car was often created in chalk lines on a garage floor. Today, the design of both chassis and engines is created and checked on a computer, before automatic transfer to production.

I could see that Ayrton Senna had anticipated these changes. In 1991, after he had won the first four races of the season, very few people were able to take him seriously when he complained that his car, his engine and his fuel were not up to the latest standards set by others.

He was, of course, entirely correct in his judgments. With a mixture of diplomacy and urgent persuasion – working in collaboration with McLaren chief Ron Dennis – he got what he wanted. From its uncompetitive position in mid-June, the McLaren-Honda returned to such a high level of performance that Ayrton was able to take advantage of several now famous mistakes and blunders by Mansell, Williams and Renault. Two crucial wins in August gave his points lead a boost. In Japan, Mansell allowed his last chance to slip away when he ran off the road. Ayrton became champion for the third time in four years.

By then, the Brazilian had already signed with McLaren and Honda for 1992. Since 1990, to the fury of Ron Dennis, he had been able to negotiate one-year contracts. He agreed to stay only when Williams barred his way to something more promising by renegotiating with Mansell and Patrese at an early stage.

When Mansell won the first five races of the 1992 season, Ayrton knew better than anyone that the Williams-Renault had a performance advantage greater than any car had enjoyed since the McLaren-Honda won 15 of its 16 races in 1988. The future at McLaren was now uncertain, with Honda on the point of withdrawing. Ayrton's mathematical chances of retaining his title were gone by mid-August. Ayrton had talks with Ferrari, but his heart was set on joining Williams and Renault for 1993. Why not? It was, after all, Frank who had first encouraged him to try an F1 car. After several apparently fruitful discussions, Frank told Ayrton that his fee was too high. Ayrton responded with typical boldness: he offered to drive for Williams in 1993 for nothing!

The alternative, he had said, would be to stop racing for one year. For a long period during the winter, it seemed that he might even be tempted to take a sabbatical year away from F1. He had no obligations and he was free to choose what to do. At the invitation of his friend Emerson Fittipaldi, he even tested a Penske IndyCar. Eventually, after testing the new Ford-engined car McLaren, he reached an agreement with Ron Dennis. At first, though, it was a race-by-race arrangement. And Ayrton's fee was so high that Dennis had to squeeze his sponsors harder than ever. To help overcome the power advantage that Williams had with the Renault V10 engine, Ron Dennis had done everything possible to ensure that Ayrton would have the most advanced McLaren ever built.

Electronically, it was such a sophisticated car that Ayrton complained about the driver's skills being "overruled" by the computer systems. I don't think he was at all happy to know that the engineers in the pits could make adjustments to items like suspension and engine settings during the race. Ayrton's 1993 season was far from over, but his eyes were probably already upon the technically superior Williams-Renault ... In 1993, Ayrton was beaten by Prost in South Africa when something went wrong in the McLaren's computer-operated "active" suspension system. In Brazil it was Ayrton's turn, but only because someone at Williams bungled a radio message to Prost, who would otherwise have surely won easily, just as he was about to switch to rain tyres in a downpour.

For Ayrton's fans, the season really came alight at Donington Park. Starting the race from fourth place on the grid, he made the very best of conditions which were atrocious throughout the weekend. The first lap of the race was memorable as he summoned up all his bravery and skill to sweep past two cars in the Craner curves, then snatching the lead from Prost at the hairpin. From there, he was unstoppable. Such astonishing driving indicated Ayrton's commitment to the team. Behind the scenes, though, he was pushing Ron Dennis to get the same Ford engines with pneumatic valves that Cosworth was supplying

It was not until the French GP that Ayrton finally signed a contract that committed him to McLaren for the whole of the 1993 season. By then he had won in Brazil, at Donington and at Monaco (a record-breaking sixth victory through those famous streets), and it looked as though he could actually challenge Prost for the title. But when the fast circuits came up on the schedule, some of the new-found enthusiasm seemed to have gone from his driving. Not only did the Williams-Renault show its superiority in the hands of both Prost and Damon Hill, but there were several races where Schumacher's Benetton-Ford was noticeably quicker. The low point of Ayrton's season, in my opinion, was when he missed his braking during the Italian GP and bunted Martin Brundle's Ligier-Renault off the road in a struggle for 7th place.

Ayrton regained some of his enthusiasm when McLaren made some modifications to the suspension and braking system of the car in time for the Portuguese GP. These were technical changes which he had been demanding for weeks, and at last they put him back ahead of Schumacher's Benetton. In the Japanese GP Ayrton had no difficulty beating Prost on a drying track sprinkled with rain, the sort of difficult conditions where he always excelled.

Afterwards came the now famous incident when he went to have a talk with Eddie Irvine in the Jordan hut behind the paddock. If he had known in advance how aggressive and tough Eddie can be, I suspect he would not have approached him. But even though this was his very first GP, Eddie refused to accept Ayrton's criticisms – and received a punch on the arm. It

was unfortunate, I think, that the incident on the track which sparked the confrontation was not picked up by Fuji TV, denying anyone else the chance to judge the situation. It has been suggested that Ayrton had had a drink when he went looking for Eddie, but it was obvious from talking to him afterwards that Ayrton felt very strongly that a new driver should have behaved less irresponsibly than Eddie had done that day.

The final race of 1993 in Adelaide was to be Ayrton's 41st victory. It was also his last. Looking back, it has to be numbered among the most magnificent of his career as he defeated the two Williams drivers on a circuit which favours good driving. Of the superiority of the Williams-Renault cars there was no doubt. Both Damon Hill and Alain Prost lapped Adelaide 0.6 seconds faster than Ayrton did, but the difference was that while the Williams drivers were unable to maintain their speed, Ayrton drove on the limit for every single one of the GP's 79 laps. He snatched the lead from Prost at the start and only gave it up briefly, to the Frenchman, during the tyre changing pit stops.

There were some emotional scenes after that race. The McLaren team manager, Ayrton's friend Jo Ramirez, was in tears below the podium. Above him, the two drivers with whom he had worked most closely in the previous ten years – Prost and Senna – were embracing each other joyfully. At last the two implacable enemies were ready to forgive and forget. They went into the post-race press conference laughing and smiling. It was a happy ending, straight out of Hollywood. But while I am sure that Prost was happy to have ended his career with a reconciliation, he would never be able to forget it had happened on Ayrton's terms. No-one could be in any doubt about who had won, and who had been obliged to accept 2nd place.

Two eras ended that afternoon in Adelaide. With his fourth world title safely in his pocket, Prost was going home into retirement after a great career. Ayrton was looking forward to the start of a new challenge, as Prost's successor, at Williams. He went straight home to Brazil, having learned from Ron Dennis that the terms of his McLaren contract would be enforced and that he would not be free to test a Williams-Renault until the new year.

A new alliance for 1988: together, Marlboro-McLaren and Honda would dominate the season, with Ayrton and his new team mate Alain Prost winning the first race (here, in Rio) and going on to success in all but one of the season's 16 Grands Prix

lboro

D by

NDA

Fate is about to snatch defeat from the jaws of victory, Monaco 1988

With its concrete walls and spine-rattling bumps, Detroit was not everyone's favourite circuit. It provided a much-needed US round in the World Championship, though, and in 1988 it gave Ayrton another victory

When Ayrton moved to McLaren in 1988, he had every reason to be apprehensive: Alain Prost had already been there for four years. It did not take the newcomer long to make friends and to build up the points that would bring him his first world driving championship

This could only be Monaco, a wonderful circuit for the photographer and, in 1988, enough action for anyone: indeed, too much incident

Top left Spa Francorchamps, victory in 1988

Top right Ferrying a team member to the pits on a moped – a Honda, of course

Centre left It was a nervous Ayrton who was escorted into Suzuka by McLaren Marketing Chief Richard West as he prepared his (successful) bid for the World Championship

Centre right and bottom left Second place only at the French GP

Bottom right With Alain Prost, discussing technicalities in 1988. The following year, they spoke to each other only through their engineers

Incredibly quickly in the groove with the new team. Hand aloft, Ayrton acknowledges the cheers of the fans after his win at the Canadian Grand Prix, 1988

Canada, 1988, and the second of Ayrton's eight victories which contributed to his first world title

The winner rejoices, Detroit 1988 (top right) – and the high point in 1988 was the championship at Suzuka, where his friend Thierry Boutsen did the honours with the champagne (centre left). Alain Prost, though, (here in Australia) had to accept that scoring more points did not make one automatically champion (bottom right)

Number 1 in the world, Ayrton's McLaren carried the reward of his 1988 championship into 1989. By the end of the year, Alain Prost was on his way to Ferrari

The uneasy alliance: Alain Prost (top, at rear) concentrates at the beginning of a qualifying session

McLaren chief Ron Dennis played scrupulously fairly with both men, supplying them with identical equipment, including personal scooters ...

A gearbox problem cost the new champion a win in Adelaide in 1988. He finished 2nd to Prost

At Monaco 1989, Ayrton won his most brilliant victory yet. Although his car had lost three gears, he maintained speed – and Prost in 2nd place did not discover until too late that by speeding up he could have won

Brazil 1989; only 11th place, an unusual result for a man who generally either finished in the top three, or didn't finish at all. Determination to stay the course bolstered, no doubt, by the home circuit location

Time-honoured view of Monaco, and time-honoured view of the race leaders throughout the 1989 season

Top right Phoenix 1989

The fateful San Marino GP of 1989: Prost (2nd, centre left) claimed that by snatching the lead on the run to the first corner, his team mate was breaking an agreement. The feud with Ayrton had started, and the Tosa hairpin incident would sour relations between the two men until August 1991

Bottom right Alongside Prost at Montreal

Xuxa de Meneghel, the hugely popular Brazilian presenter of a children's TV show, who shared Ayrton's life for almost a year

Attacking Prost for the lead at Suzuka in 1989 ... and being pushed off the track as he tries a legitimate passing move at the chicane ... Prost steps out in the belief that with Ayrton also out, his championship is safe. Ayrton continued, stopped for a new nose cone — and still finished first. The win was taken away, a contentious decision that exercises F1 cognoscenti even today

Winning at Monaco is always special – and Ayrton did it a record six times ...

... Of course, you need a lot of help – as shown by the 14 engineers and mechanics in this shot alone

The 1990 German GP, checking the mirror on the way to another victory in July at Hockenheim

Behind the scenes and a few rare moments of inactivity inside the McLaren garage. Ayrton would often stay with the mechanics until late, watching, asking questions and learning more about his car

Retirement in Australia, 1990

A new season, 1990, Monaco, and a new team mate ...

... Gerhard Berger would probably have been a closer competitor for Ayrton if he had been smaller and therefore more comfortable in the car. They soon became genuine friends, though – and Ayrton was to be champion for the second time. Spa (top right); Monaco (centre left)

Monza 1990

Victory for the third year in succession at Monaco in May, 1991

An appointment with destiny at Interlagos. Ayrton was proud of his victories at Monaco, but I don't think any of them meant as much to him as his 1991 win in front of the home crowd in Sao Paulo. Here he sets off with fresh tyres during practice

Rounding the Loews hairpin at Monaco in 1991

Semi-automatic gearbox on display at Hungary, 1991

The 1991 season was to be a struggle with the technically superior Williams-Renault of Nigel Mansell. But with the help of Berger, Honda and his loyal fans, Ayrton was to be champion for the third and last time. Victories in the San Marino GP (top right) and in Brazil (centre left)

Coming into the seafront chicane at Monaco in 1991, Ayrton's fourth victory in the classic Grand Prix

The Prince of Monaco. Ayrton made it his home when he was in Europe; (Michael Schumacher was a neighbour)

Into the Loews hairpin once more: 78 laps and two hours to victory

Third place in Mexico, 1991

My favourite shot of Ayrton, as I will always remember him. I got this faceful of champagne at Spa in 1991, as he celebrated a great win in the Belgian GP

The master celebrates at Phoenix in 1991, the last Grand Prix to be held in the USA before his death

Even though Ayrton would win the first four GPs of the 1991 season, including Imola (top) and a third consecutive victory at Monaco (opposite), he knew that McLaren and Honda would have to work hard to stay ahead of
the ever-stronger challenge from Mansell, Williams and Renault. The facial expressions on the podium at Monaco
(above, centre left) say a lot -- and Ayrton was soon voicing his concern to friends like Bernie Ecclestone (centre
right) that McLaren and Honda could not afford to relax. Although he ran out of fuel at Silverstone, where he got
a taste of Renault power after thumbing a lift from Mansell (bottom left), he was much happier with the virtually
new Honda V12, seen spitting flame in qualifying at Hockenheim (bottom right)

An unforgettable moment of the 1991 season was the famous wheel-to-wheel duel during the Spanish GP (top) when Mansell dared to drive past Ayrton. Mansell's Championship hopes vanished when he spun off in Suzuka -- and Ayrton ended the year by defeating his rival in the rain-shortened 14-lap sprint at Adelaide (above)

At Suzuka, Berger led until just before the tyre stops, when they changed position. On instructions from his pit by radio, Ayrton pulled off on the last lap and gave the race to his Austrian team mate. Although Gerhard expressed his gratitude, I know that both men regarded it as an unsatisfactory outcome. Ron Dennis (below), Adelaide

Ayrton equalled Graham Hill's record at Monaco by winning a fifth GP through the streets of the Principality -- but only because Nigel Mansell had to make an unscheduled pit stop when a wheel came loose with seven laps to go

The last three laps of the race, with Mansell on four fresh Goodyears itching to find a way past Ayrton on his worn rubber, were perhaps the most exciting that have ever been seen at Monaco. Somehow, Ayrton always managed to fill the exact piece of road that Nigel wanted

With Honda winding down its FI involvement, and with Mansell and Williams-Renault in the ascendant, 1992 was a disaster by Ayrton's standards. While Mansell won the first five GPs, Ayrton retired at home in Brazil (top) and didn't really need the police protection at Imola! Monaco (centre right) was one of his only three wins -- but he was finding a firm friend in his team mate Gerhard Berger (bottom left)

There was lots for Ayrton to think about at the Hungarian GP in 1992, for although he won the race his victory was forgotten in the euphoria that surrounded Nigel Mansell's world championship, clinched with a fighting 2nd place. Their old antagonism was forgotten in the emotion on the podium. After his transmission failed during the British GP, Ayrton spent a few moments on his knees at Club corner. In spite of the reverence, this was not his luckiest place: he pulled off to retire at exactly the same spot in three consecutive years!

Storm clouds at Estoril in 1992 (left) as Ayrton laps a slower competitor. It was to be his worst season since joining McLaren in 1988 and he was thinking about switching to IndyCar racing: during the winter he even tested a Penske (above). Meanwhile, there were grateful farewells to be made to Honda at Suzuka (top)

Always popular in Japan, Ayrton waves to the loyal fans as he enters the pitlane at Suzuka, after defeating Prost's Williams-Renault to win the 1993 Grand Prix

The 1993 season started with no full commitment from Ayrton that he would do a full season with McLaren. But there was no doubt that he would race in Brazil, where he won a superb tactical victory. Third man Michael Schumacher lingers with him (left) on the podium. Ayrton did well in South Africa to finish 2nd to Prost (top), despite suspension troubles. Donington Park and Monaco (centre) produced brilliant victories and after a mid-season slump he won again in Japan and Australia (bottom). It was good to see him reconciled with Alain Prost on the podium at Adelaide

Although rain helped Ayrton to overcome Damon Hill's power advantage in the 1993 Brazilian GP, the Englishman's Williams-Renault was long gone at Spa (top). He was often a solitary figure, but Ayrton enjoyed a chat with Michael Schumacher as they walked to the drivers' briefing before the British GP

Opportunities for group photos at Adelaide 1993: the FIA gets the drivers together (top) and the McLaren boys have their last chance to be pictured with Ayrton (above). I hate this type of shot because there is always some-one who decides not to look at the camera ...

Williams, 1994

It was a bright, cold afternoon in January 1994 when Ayrton at last drove a Williams. The team had a new sponsor, Rothmans cigarettes, and the media attention was almost overwhelming. .

Under the press questioning, Ayrton said all the right things about his new career. He reminded everyone that it had been Frank Williams, back in 1983, who gave him his first chance to test an F1 car. He complimented Renault on the power of the V10 engine. He said he looked forward to having Damon Hill as his team mate. What went unspoken was his anxiety about the team's new car, the FW16, which would not be ready until a couple of weeks before the first race in Brazil. Patrick Head, the Williams designer, was suggesting that the later the new car appeared, the more up-to-date would be its aerodynamic specification. I think that Ayrton wanted to see how well Williams had adapted the new FW16 to the FIA's ban on electronic aids.

When at last he tried the FW16, at Silverstone in early March, there were surprisingly few people present. It was a typically horrid Silverstone day, cold and wet.. Everything was low-key. Many times before, Ayrton had tested a new car here – and had been able to analyse its qualities almost immediately. Here, there was no mistaking the black look on his face after his first couple of runs. He wasn't happy with his new car, and he didn't believe he was going to like it until some major changes had been made. His dissatisfaction was not just in the behaviour of the car but in the driving position, especially the steering wheel, vertically mounted instead of being angled with the bottom closer to him.

In the few days left before the car had to be put on a plane for Sao Paulo, Ayrton did not hesitate to slam the FW16. It was particularly bad, he said, over the bumps in the surface of the tarmac for which Interlagos is famous. His fears were justified in qualifying, when it took a tremendous act of bravery to get him round his home circuit faster than Michael Schumacher.

With the eyes of his countrymen upon him, Ayrton made a wonderful effort in the race by taking the lead at the first corner and holding off Schumacher for 22 laps, until the first pit stops. This year, for the first time since 1983, refuelling was allowed, and there was tension in the pit lane, where the working personnel were dressed in fireproof uniforms. Ayrton entered the pits narrowly in front of Schumacher. When the stops were complete, the Benetton driver was ahead. Driving on the limit, Ayrton struggled hard to keep up with the new leader. But he was obviously in trouble. Fifteen laps from the finish, he spun sideways, stalled the engine and had to abandon his car.

Had the Williams pit work been inferior? Had Schumacher benefited from the Ford engine's lower fuel consumption? Or had there been some other factor? There were no definite answers. It was only later in the year, when Benetton was accused by the FIA of illegally removing the filter from a refuelling nozzle at Hockenheim, that doubts resurfaced. In effect, Interlagos was to be his last race. Three weeks later he competed in the Asian GP at the Aida circuit in Japan, only to spin off at the first corner in a collision with Hakkinen, while vainly chasing Schumacher again. On May 1, while leading Schumacher in the third round at Imola, he was to die at the Tamburello corner.

My memories of that horrific weekend started happily, on Thursday, when Ayrton was visited in the paddock by Rubens Barrichello and Christian Fittipaldi. My picture of the three Brazilians shows them smiling and laughing as they talked together. On Friday afternoon, Ayrton was at the side of Rubens as the Jordan-Hart driver was carried into the medical centre after a tremendous crash during qualifying. Although Rubens' injuries proved remarkably light, the accident clearly worried Ayrton. Then, on Saturday, Roland Ratzenberger went off the road at one of the fastest points on the circuit and ran almost head-on into a concrete wall. Ayrton saw the impact on the monitor in the McLaren pit, and again he wanted – he insisted – on being at the scene. When he returned, he locked himself into the motorhome. There were reports, later, that he had some sort of premonition about himself, although I find such suggestions difficult to believe.

Nevertheless, it was a serious-looking Ayrton who went to the track for Sunday's race. One of his close friends lay injured in hospital, and another popular driver was dead. When I spoke weeks later to Joseph Leberer, the Austrian physiotherapist who had worked as Ayrton's personal trainer for the previous three years, I learned that Ayrton was very uneasy.

It is not my role to go through what happened that day. The world's TV stations carried the scene in all its horror. It was an afternoon when I suddenly lost interest in being at Imola, in motor racing and in being a photographer.

Overleaf Williams' new FW16 for the 1994 season wasn't ready until a test day at Silverstone on February 24. Ayrton described its handling characteristics over bumps as "uncomfortable," perhaps because it was designed to run so close to the ground that it struck enough sparks to light up a grey afternoon

Alone with his thoughts at the Pacific Grand Prix, Japan, 17 April, 1994

Interlagos 1994: Sao Paulo's "Mr Mayor," Paulo Maluf, seems to be showing Ayrton how to use the McLaren's gearshift (above). The local driver led the first part of the Brazilian GP from Alesi and Schumacher (right) and was struggling to stay with Schumacher's Benetton when he spun off

Ayrton never forgot Frank Williams' generosity in letting him test his car in 1983: he had warm feelings for Frank and appeared ready to work in harmony with new team mate Damon Hill (top). Looking thoughtful before the Pacific GP at Aida in April (centre), his race finished in a collision at the first corner. Then it was to Imola, and a lighthearted conversation on Thursday with Rubens Barrichello, his protege and fellow Paulista

Imola, May 1, 1994 (top): the race has been neutralised following a startline collision and Ayrton leads the field behind the pace car as the track is cleaned up. He was still leading when he crashed on the second lap of the restarted race. Three weeks later, at Monaco (above), his fellow drivers lined up to pay their silent tribute

FOURTEEN YEARS WITH
AYRTON SENNA

1981

1982

1983

1984

1985

1986

1987

1988

1989

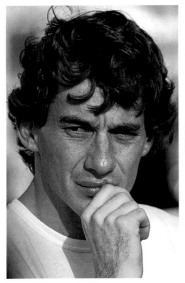

1990

1991

1992

1993

1994

AYRTON SENNA CAREER RECORD

KART CHAMPIONSHIP WINS:
1977-1978   South American Championship
1976-1981   Brazilian Championship

KART WORLD CHAMPIONSHIP POSITIONS
1977 - 6th
1979 - 2nd
1980 - 2nd
1981 - 4th

1981

ENTRANT: Van Diemen

Pos	Race	Date	Circuit
	CAR: Van Diemen RF80-Ford		
5	P&O Ferries FF1600, round 1	1.3.81	Brands Hatch
	CAR: Van Diemen R81-Ford		
3	Townsend-Thoresen FF1600, r.1	8.3.81	Thruxton
1	Townsend-Thoresen FF1600, r.2	15.3.81	Brands Hatch
2	Townsend-Thoresen FF1600, r.3	22.3.81	Mallory Park
2	Townsend-Thoresen FF1600, r.4	5.4.81	Mallory Park
2	Townsend-Thoresen FF1600, r.5	3.5.81	Snetterton
1	RAC FF1600, r.1	24.5.81	Oulton Park
1	Townsend-Thoresen FF1600, r.6	25.5.81	Mallory Park
1	Townsend-Thoresen FF1600, r.7	7.6.81	Snetterton
2	RAC FF1600, r.2	21.6.81	Silverstone
1	Townsend-Thoresen FF1600, r.8	27.6.81	Oulton Park
1	RAC FF1600, r.3	4.7.81	Donington Park
4	RAC FF1600, r. 4	12.7.81	Brands Hatch
1	Townsend-Thoresen FF1600, r 9	25.7.81	Oulton Park
1	RAC FF1600, r. 5	26.7.81	Mallory Park
1	Townsend-Thoresen FF1600, r.10	2.8.81	Brands Hatch
1	RAC FF1600, r. 6	9.8.81	Snetterton
1	Townsend-Thoresen FF1600, r.11	15.8.81	Donington Park
1	Townsend-Thoresen FF1600, r.12	31.8.81	Thruxton
2	Townsend-Thoresen FF1600, r.13	29.9.81	Brands Hatch

1982

ENTRANT: Rushen Green Racing – except 13.11.82/Thruxton: W. Surrey Racing
CAR: Van Diemen RF82-Ford - except 30.5.82/Oulton Park: Sunbeam Talbot T1 and 13.11.82/Thruxton: Ralt RT3-Toyota

Pos	Race	Date	Circuit
1	Pace British FF2000, r.1	7.3.82	Brands Hatch
1	Pace British FF2000, r.2	27.3.82	Oulton Park
1	Pace British FF2000, r.3	28.3.82	Silverstone
1	Pace British FF2000, r.4	4.4.82	Donington Park
1	Pace British FF2000, r. 5	9.4.82	Snetterton
1	Pace British FF2000, r. 6	12.4.82	Silverstone
ret	EFDA FF2000, r.1	18.4.82	Zolder
1	EFDA FF2000, r.2	2.5.82	Donington Park
1	Pace British FF2000, r. 7	2.5.82	Mallory Park
ret	EFDA FF2000, r.3	9.5.82	Zolder
ret	Pace British FF2000, r. 8	30.5.82	Oulton Park
1	Celebrity Race	30.5.82	Oulton Park
1	Pace British FF2000, r. 9	31.5.82	Brands Hatch
1	Pace British FF2000, r. 10	6.6.82	Mallory Park
1	Pace British FF2000, r. 11	13.6.82	Brands Hatch
ret	EFDA FF2000, r.4	20.6.82	Hockenheim
1	Pace British FF2000, r. 12	26.6.82	Oulton Park
1	EFDA FF2000, r.5	3.7.82	Zandvoort
2	Pace British FF2000, r. 13	4.7.82	Snetterton
1	Pace British FF2000, r. 14	10.7.82	Castle Combe
1	Pace British FF2000, r. 15	1.8.82	Snetterton
1	EFDA FF2000, r. 6	8.8.82	Hockenheim
1	EFDA FF2000, r. 7	15.8.82	Osterreichring
1	EFDA FF2000, r. 8	22.8.82	Jyllandsring
1	Pace British FF2000, r. 16	30.8.82	Thruxton
1	Pace British FF2000, r. 17	5.9.82	Silverstone
1	EFDA FF2000, r. 9	12.9.82	Mondello Park
2	Pace British FF2000, r. 20	26.9.82	Brands Hatch
1	Formula 3 Race	13.11.82	Thruxton

1983

ENTRANT: West Surrey Racing – except 20.10.83/Macau GP: Marlboro/Teddy Yip
CAR: Ralt RT3-Toyota

Pos	Race	Date	Circuit
1	Marlboro British F3, round 1	6.3.83	Silverstone
1	Marlboro British F3, round 2	13.3.83	Thruxton
1	Marlboro British F3, round 3	20.3.83	Silverstone
1	Marlboro British F3, round 4	27.3.83	Donington Park
1	Marlboro British F3, round 5	4.4.83	Thruxton
1	Marlboro British F3, round 6	24.4.83	Silverstone
1	Marlboro British F3, round 7	2.5.83	Thruxton
1	Marlboro British F3, round 8	8.5.83	Brands Hatch
1	Marlboro British F3, round 9	30.5.83	Silverstone
ret	Marlboro British F3, round 10	12.6.83	Silverstone
dns	Marlboro British F3, round 11	19.6.83	Cadwell Park
ret	Marlboro British F3, round 12	3.7.83	Snetterton
1	Marlboro British F3, round 13	16.7.83	Silverstone
2	Marlboro British F3, round 14	24.7.83	Donington Park
ret	Marlboro British F3, round 15	6.8.83	Oulton Park
1	Marlboro British F3, round 16	29.8.83	Silverstone
ret	Marlboro British F3, round 17	11.9.83	Oulton Park
ret	Marlboro British F3, round 18	18.9.83	Thruxton
2	Marlboro British F3, round 19	2.10.83	Silverstone
1	Macau GP	20.10.83	Macau
1	Marlboro British F3, round 20	27.10.83	Thruxton

1984

ENTRANT: Toleman Group Motorsport - except
12.5.84/Nurburgring: Daimler Benz AG and 15.7.84/Nurburgring:
Reinhold Joest Racing Team

Pos	Race	Date	Circuit

CAR: Toleman TG 183B-Hart)

Pos	Race	Date	Circuit
ret	Brazilian GP	25.3.84	Rio
6	South African GP	7.4.84	Kyalami
6	Belgian GP	29.4.84	Zolder
dnq	San Marino GP	6.5.84	Imola

CAR: Mercedes-Benz 190E

1	Inaugural Saloon Car Race	12.5.84	Nürburgring

CAR: Toleman TG 184-Hart

ret	French GP	20.5.84	Dijon
2	Monaco GP	3.6.84	Monte Carlo
7	Canadian GP	17.6.84	Montreal
ret	Detroit GP	24.6.84	Detroit
ret	Dallas GP	8.7.84	Dallas

CAR: Porsche 956

8	Nürburgring 1000km	15.7.84	Nürburgring

CAR: Toleman TG 184-Hart

3	British GP	22.7.84	Brands Hatch
ret	German GP	5.8.84	Hockenheim
ret	Austrian	19.8.84	Osterreichring
ret	Dutch GP	26.8.84	Zandvoort
dns	Italian GP	9.9.84	Monza
ret	European GP	7.10.84	Nürburgring
3	Portuguese GP	21.10.84	Estoril

1985

ENTRANT: John Player Team Lotus
CAR: Lotus 97T-Renault

Pos	Race	Date	Circuit
ret	Brazilian GP	25.3.85	Rio
1	Portuguese GP	21.4.85	Estoril
7/ret	San Marino GP	5.5.85	Imola
ret	Monaco GP	19.5.85	Monte Carlo
16	Canadian GP	16.6.85	Montreal
ret	Detroit	23.6.85	Detroit
ret	French GP	7.7.85	Paul Ricard
10	British GP	21.7.85	Silverstone
ret	German GP	4.8.85	Nürburgring
2.	Austrian GP	18.8.85	Osterreichring
3	Dutch GP	25.8.85	Zandvoort
3	Italian GP	8.9.85	Monza
1	Belgian GP	15.9.85	Spa
2	European GP	6.10.85	Brands Hatch
ret	South African GP	19.10.85	Kyalami
ret	Australian GP	3.11.85	Adelaide

1986

ENTRANT: John Player Team Lotus
CAR: Lotus 98T-Renault

Pos	Race	Date	Circuit
2	Brazilian GP	23.3.86	Rio
1	Spanish GP	13.4.86	Jerez
ret	San Marino GP	27.4.86	Imola
3	Monaco GP	11.5.86	Monte Carlo
2	Belgian GP	25.5.86	Spa
5	Canadian GP	15.6.86	Montreal
1	Detroit GP	22.6.86	Detroit
ret	French GP	6.7.86	Paul Ricard
ret	British GP	13.7.86	Brands Hatch
2	German GP	27.7.86	Hockenheim
2	Hungarian GP	10.8.86	Hungaroring
ret	Austrian GP	17.8.86	Osterreichring
ret	Italian GP	7.9.86	Monza
4	Portuguese GP	17.8.86	Estoril
3	Mexican GP	12.10.86	Mexico City
ret	Australian GP	26.10.86	Adelaide

1987

ENTRANT: Camel Team Lotus Honda
CAR: Lotus 99T-Honda

Pos	Race	Date	Circuit
ret	Brazilian GP	12.4.87	Rio
2	San Marino GP	3.5.87	Imola
ret	Belgian GP	17.5.87	Spa
5	Canadian GP	15.6.87	Montreal
1	Detroit GP	22.6.87	Detroit
4	French GP	5.7.87	Paul Ricard
3	British GP	12.7.87	Brands Hatch
3	German GP	26.7.87	Hockenheim
2	Hungarian GP	9.8.87	Hungaroring
5	Austrian GP	16.8.87	Osterreichring
2	Italian GP	6.9.87	Monza
7	Portuguese GP	20.9.87	Estoril
5	Spanish GP	27.9.87	Jerez
ret	Mexican GP	18.10.87	Mexico City
2	Japanese GP	1.11.87	Suzuka
dsq	Australian GP	15.11.87	Adelaide

continued overleaf

1988

ENTRANT: Honda Marlboro McLaren
CAR: McLaren MP 4/4-Honda

Pos	Race	Date	Circuit
dsq	Brazilian GP	3.4.88	Rio
I	San Marino GP	1.5.88	Imola
ret	Monaco GP	15.5.88	Monte Carlo
2	Mexican GP	29.5.88	Mexico City
I	Canadian GP	12.6.88	Montreal
I	Detroit GP	19.6.88	Detroit
2	French GP	3.7.88	Paul Ricard
I	British GP	10.7.88	Silverstone
I	German GP	24.7.88	Hockenheim
I	Hungarian GP	8.8.88	Hungaroring
I	Belgian GP	28.8.88	Spa
ret	Italian GP	11.9.88	Monza
6	Portuguese GP	25.9.88	Estoril
4	Spanish GP	2.10.88	Jerez
I	Japanese GP	30.10.88	Suzuka
2	Australian GP	13.11.88	Adelaide

1989

ENTRANT: Honda Marlboro McLaren
CAR: McLaren MP4/5-Honda

Pos	Race	Date	Circuit
11	Brazilian GP	26.3.89	Rio
I	San Marino GP	23.4.89	Imola
I	Monaco GP	7.5.89	Monte Carlo
I	Mexican GP	28.5.89	Mexico City
ret	US PG (Phoenix)	4.6.89	Phoenix
7/ret	Canadian GP	18.6.89	Montreal
ret	French GP	9.7.89	Paul Ricard
ret	British GP	16.7.89	Silverstone
I	German GP	30.7.89	Hockenheim
2	Hungarian GP	13.8.89	Hungaroring
I	Belgian GP	27.8.89	Spa
ret	Italian GP	10.9.89	Monza
ret	Portuguese GP	24.9.89	Estoril
I	Spanish GP	1.10.89	Jerez
dsq	Japanese GP	22.10.89	Suzuka
ret	Australian GP	5.11.89	Adelaide

1990

ENTRANT: Honda Marlboro McLaren
CAR: McLaren MP4/5B-Honda

Pos	Race	Date	Circuit
I	US GP (Phoenix)	11.3.90	Phoenix
3	Brazilian GP	25.3.90	Interlagos
ret	San Marino GP	13.5.90	Imola
I	Monaco GP	27.5.90	Monte Carlo
I	Canadian GP	10.6.90	Monteal
20/ret	Mexican GP	24.6.90	Mexico City
3	French GP	8.7.90	Paul Ricard
3	British GP	15.7.90	Silverstone
I	German GP	29.7.90	Hockenheim
2	Hungarian GP	12.8.90	Hungaroring
I	Belgian GP	26.8.90	Spa
I	Italian GP	9.9.90	Monza
2	Portuguese GP	23.9.90	Estoril
ret	Spanish GP	30.9.90	Jerez
ret	Japanese GP	21.10.90	Suzuka
ret	Australian GP	4.11.90	Adelaide

1991

ENTRANT: Honda Marlboro McLaren
CAR: McLaren MP4/6-Honda

Pos	Race	Date	Circuit
I	US PG	10.3.91	Phoenix
I	Brazilian GP	24.3.91	Interlagos
I	San Marino GP	28.4.91	Imola
I	Monaco GP	12.5.91	Monte Carlo
ret	Canadian GP	2.6.91	Montreal
3	Mexican GP	16.6.91	Mexico City
3	French GP	7.7.91	Magny-Cours
4/ret	British GP	14.7.91	Silverstone
7/ret	German GP	28.7.91	Hockenheim
I	Hungarian GP	11.8.91	Hungaroring
I	Belgian GP	25.8.91	Spa
2	Italian GP	8.9.91	Monza
2	Portuguese GP	22.9.91	Estoril
5	Spanish GP	10.10.91	Barcelona
2	Japanese GP	10.10.91	Suzuka
I	Australian GP	3.11.91	Adelaide

1992

ENTRANT: Honda Marlboro McLaren

Pos	Race	Date	Circuit
CAR: MP4/6B-Honda			
3	South African GP	1.3.92	Kyalami
ret	Mexican GP	22.3.92	Mexico City
CAR: MP4/7-Honda			
ret	Brazilian GP	5.4.92	Brazil
9/ret	Spanish GP	3.5.92	Barcelona
3	San Marino GP	17.5.92	Imola
I	Monaco GP	31.5.92	Monte Carlo
ret	Canadian	14.6.92	Montreal
ret	French GP	5.7.92	Magny-Cours
ret	British GP	12.7.92	Silverstone
2	German GP	26.7.92	Hockenheim
I	Hungarian GP	16.8.92	Budapest
5	Belgium GP	30.8.92	Spa-Francorchamps
I	Italian GP	13.9.92	Monza
3	Portuguese GP	27.9.92	Estoril
ret	Japanese GP	25.10.92	Suzuka
ret	Australian GP	8.11.92	Adelaide

1993

ENTRANT: Honda Marlboro McLaren
CAR: MP4/8 Ford

Pos	Race	Date	Circuit
2	South African GP	14.3.93	Kyalami
1	Brazilian GP	28.3.93	Sao Paulo
1	European GP	11.4.93	Donington Park
ret	San Marino GP	25.4.93	Imola
2	Spanish GP	9.5.93	Barcelona
1	Monaco GP	23.5.93	Monte Carlo
18	Canadian GP	13.6.93	Montreal
4	French GP	4.7.93	Magny-Cours
5	British GP	11.7.93	Silverstone
4	German GP	25.7.93	Hockenheim
ret	Hungarian GP	15.8.93	Budapest
4	Belgium GP	29.8.93	Spa-Francorchamps
ret	Italian GP	12.9.93	Monza
ret	Portuguese GP	26.9.93	Estoril
1	Japanese GP	24.10.93	Suzuka
1	Australian GP	7.11.93	Adelaide

1994

ENTRANT: Williams
CAR: FW16-Renault

Pos	Race	Date	Circuit
ret	Brazilian GP	27.3.94	Sao Paulo
ret	Pacific GP	17.4.94	Aida, Japan
fatal	San Marino GP	1.5.94	Imola

Below How it all began: South American kart champion twice, second in the the World Championship in 1979 and 1980

Championship records

Formula 1 World Championship placings
1st-6th + pole + fastest lap

Races	161
1st	41
2nd	23
3rd	16
4th	7
5th	6
6th	3
pole	65
Fastest lap	19
Failed to qualify	1

Formula 1 positions

1984	9th
1985	4th
1986	4th
1987	3rd
1988	1st
1989	2nd
1990	1st
1991	1st
1992	4th
1993	2nd

Other Motor Racing Championship wins

1981	RAC FF-1600
1981	Townsend-Thoresen FF1600 Champion
1982	Pace British FF2000 Champion
1982	EFDA FF2000 Champion
1983	Marlboro British F3 Champion

Ayrton Senna Da Silva, RIP

"At the beginning, I was just doing it for the feeling of driving: I liked the feeling of moving the steering wheel, braking, putting on the power, feeling the engine, listening to the engine, feeling the air on my face, the speed. It got to me when I was a kid: it got inside me, and stayed there.

I had a fantastic childhood, because I was very free to play. I had to go to school every day for half the day, but the other half of the day I had free to play all sorts of games with my friends. And we were in an open area, we were safe, we were healthy - which meant we could play all kinds of different games. My family has always been very united. My parents always gave me really good advice. When I did good things they gave me good words, and they directed me to the right things, whatever was necessary. So I was a very fortunate child. I went to a very good school, and had a proper education. Basically I was always doing what I liked to do. Healthy things, but I was enjoying them because it was what I wanted to do. All of that mixed with go-karting, because that was my hobby. It was incredible fun for me, but that was only on Sunday afternoons.

And in that period I was not doing so well at school, because the go-kart was taking over. My mother would say, "you do not go-kart until you do better scores at school". So I stopped until I got better scores, and then again I had the go-kart on Sunday afternoon.

The only motivation to make you go race after race, travel after travel is winning .... The possibility that you have for winning. If you don't have that, nothing else can make you work.

It's something that is very lonely in a way, because once you get in a car, on a circuit, it is yourself and the car, the situation is extremely absorbing, and perhaps because I have experienced on many occasions the feeling of finding new things - even thought "ok that is my maximum" - then suddenly I always found something extra. That process is something almost non-stop in terms of excitement and motivation. I only knew one way of doing it. And I've been doing it for many years, not just in Formula One., but as you know, in the racing I did before, just the same. If you've done it that way over a period, working hard, with the perserverance, determination, hard work - continuously, keeping going - there's no other way of doing it.

Perhaps a motivating factor for me is the discoveries that I keep having, every time I am driving. When I push, I go and I find something more. I go again and I find something more. That is perhaps the most fascinating motivating factor for me. The challenge of doing better.

And in the process of learning how to live with it, you of course have extraordinary feelings and emotions when you get near to an accident or a feeling that - uh!- you were just almost gone [over the limit]. It's fascinating in a way. It's attractive in a way. But it's a challenge for you to control it and not exceed those things. So the feeling of living in that band, which I think is very narrow, between overdoing and being too easy, is very small. The challenge to remain within that band as much as possible is very much a motivation. It takes a lot from you to maintain sharpness. At the same time, you should have no fear. Because if you have fear, you cannot commit yourself. It's important to know what it [fear] is, because it will keep you more switched on, keep you more sharp. It will determine on many occasions, your limits.

These things bring you to reality as to how fragile you are; at the same moment you are doing something that nobody else is able to do. The same moment that you are seen as the best, the fastest and somebody that cannot be touched, you are enormously fragile. Because in a split second, it's gone. These two extremes are feelings that you don't get every day. These are all things which contribute to - how can I say - knowing yourself deeper and deeper. These are things that keep me going. To be competitive as long as I can. Which means to be well physically and in mind, to perform and exploit my potential and learn this as well. To be in the right place, so I can develop my potential and be competitve. And that is as long as I drive, and every time I drive. That is my goal, because now, as you say, I have won races, I have won championships. I can only repeat those things. OK it is the first time that you have done it, that is fine. But when you have broken some records, another record is no big deal. I will tell you one thing: it took me 10 years of Formula One to win three championships. It would not be easy, and I know how hard it is because I did it.

If I ever happen to have an accident that eventually costs me my life, I hope it is in one go. I would not like to be in a wheelchair. I would not like to be in hospital suffering from whatever injury it was. If I am going to live, I want to live fully. Very intensely, because I am an intense person. It would ruin my life if I had to live partially."

(Reproduced with the kind permission of Russell Bulgin and **Car** magazine)